Wonderfully Made

A Daily Devotional For Eating Disorder Recovery

CAITLYN HOERNER

ISBN: 198384019X
ISBN-13: 978-1983840197

ACKNOWLEDGMENTS

To my incredible treatment team, my always supportive family, and the countless others who have helped make my recovery, and this book, possible-- thank you for believing in me.

INTRODUCTION

"I want God on my treatment team."

Those are the words I spoke to my pastor one cold Sunday morning after church. I was lost, scared, and frankly desperate. Years of treatment for my eating disorder had saved me from the physical destruction I had done, but no matter how hard I tried, I continued to fall back into those habits time again. I had (what I would argue as) the best treatment team in the state, but something was missing, and I felt it in my soul. I would love to say that giving myself to God that day caused an instant and miraculous turnaround, but it still took work. Like any relationship, I had to learn to communicate with Him, spend time with Him, and ultimately call upon Him when I felt too weak to carry on.

While no substitute for professional help, my hope is that this book may serve as an introduction to invite God on *your* treatment team as well. Restoring physical and emotional health during and after an eating disorder is of utmost importance, but so is addressing the damage that has been done to the spirit. In my experience, long-term recovery depends on proper nutrition, correcting emotional and physiological imbalances, and working towards good spiritual health. Please refer to the resources page at the back of the book to find support and information about eating disorder recovery, and remember, you are *wonderfully made*.

Day One

"I PRAISE YOU FOR I AM FEARFULLY AND WONDERFULLY MADE." —PSALM 139:14

God made you one of a kind. You are His creation, His work of art. Think of a time you created a painting. Now imagine showing it off, so proud of your work, only for it to be critiqued and scrutinized harshly. Not so fun, huh? Do you think God feels those same pains when we criticize and bash on our bodies? They are His handiwork, after all. Are we downplaying His role as the Creator of all things good? How do you think He views you?

Dear God, thank You for creating me as I am. Thank You for breathing life into me so that I can experience the good You have planned for me. Please open my eyes so that I may see myself the way You do, as Your beautiful creation. Teach me to appreciate my body for all it can do, not by how it looks.

Activity: *Really* get to know this verse. Write it down as plainly or as decoratively as you desire. Tape it to your mirror so you see it when you feel tempted to bash your body. Don't *ever* let yourself forget this verse.

_____

_____

_____

_____

_____

_____

_____

_____

_____

_____

_____

_____

_____

_____

_____

_____

_____

_____

_____

_____

_____

_____

_____

_____

Day Two

"DO NOT CONFORM TO THE PATTERN OF THIS WORLD, BUT BE TRANSFORMED BY THE RENEWING OF YOUR MIND."

—ROMANS 12:2

It can be so difficult to maintain a healthy body image in today's society. With the media constantly bombarding us with images and products targeting our greatest insecurities, it's no wonder so few people are satisfied with their appearances! Apart from being physically unrealistic, these "beauty standards" totally discredit the idea that we are made as unique individuals. We as Christians are called to show God's love not only to others, but to ourselves. Talk about a tough mission! By transforming our thoughts to show love for ourselves, we have the ability to serve as role models for our brother, sisters, friends, and total strangers. Radical self-acceptance, while frowned upon by a society driven by insecurities, can be a vessel for change in our broken world. *You* can be that change.

✝

God, give me the strength and the graces to accept my body as it is- not as society would have it. Show me the beauty You see in every inch of me. Allow me the courage to reject society's idea of "beauty" so that I may better appreciate the intrinsic beauty and divinity granted to me by being Your daughter.

Activity: Identify the worldly sources of insecurities in your life. Do pictures of models cause you to feel inadequate? Perhaps it may be time to cancel that fashion magazine subscription. Is it the scale in the bathroom? Try hiding it from yourself for a few days. Eliminating these triggers may help you rely less on the world's idea of "beauty" so that you can better appreciate your own.

_____

_____

_____

_____

_____

_____

_____

_____

_____

_____

_____

_____

_____

_____

_____

_____

_____

_____

_____

_____

_____

Day Three

> "'FOR IT DOESN'T GO INTO THEIR HEART BUT INTO THEIR STOMACH, AND THEN OUT OF THE BODY.' IN SAYING THIS, JESUS DECLARED ALL FOODS CLEAN." —MARK 7:19

Admittedly, I take this a bit out of context. In this section of scripture, Jesus denounces the strict dietary laws outlined in the Old Testament. (We, however, can interpret this as admonishing the ridiculous "rules" our eating disorders create to control our eating). Jesus emphasizes in verse 14 that it matters more what comes out of you than what goes in. He says, "Nothing outside a person can defile them by going into them. Rather, it is what comes out of a person that defiles them." In other words, the occasional candy bar or pack of chips won't make you a bad person. What *should* cause you guilt, however, is unkind words or deeds against His children… yourself included!

Lord, thank You for the freedom You offer me from the chains of my disordered eating habits. Give me the courage to reach toward Your promises of health and happiness. Free me from the guilt and shame I associate with certain foods, so that I may spend more energy glorifying You.

Activity: Identify foods that trigger you to binge, purge, restrict, or that otherwise cause you struggles with disordered eating. Know that God has intended this to nourish your body, not do harm to it. Have a loved one sit with you as you challenge yourself to conquer this food when you are ready.

Day Four

"MY GRACE IS SUFFICIENT FOR YOU, FOR MY POWER IS MADE PERFECT IN WEAKNESS." –2 CORINTHIANS 12:9

We are weak. It's a very difficult thing for us to admit. We can't do it all, no matter how hard we try. But here's a secret- God can. When we try to do things on our own, we often fall short. We might rely on unhealthy coping mechanisms to pull us out of a struggle, when in fact, we're actually digging ourselves deeper. God tells us we don't need that. We need *Him* and *His* grace. He is enough when we aren't. His graces will pull us through- All we have to do is ask!

Lord God, thank You for Your undying love and everlasting grace. In times of struggle, help me remember to call upon Your Name as opposed to my old ways of coping. Give me the courage to push further in my trials so that I may one day succeed.

Activity: Dedicate something in your life to be your "Savior sign"- that when your eyes land on it, you immediately think of God and His love and grace. This could be a favorite piece of jewelry, a landmark you pass by frequently, or even that freckle that makes you one-of-a-kind. Let this be a gentle reminder to ask for the day's graces.

_____

_____

_____

_____

_____

_____

_____

_____

_____

_____

_____

_____

_____

_____

_____

_____

_____

_____

_____

_____

Day Five

"CHARM IS DECEPTIVE, AND BEAUTY IS FLEETING; BUT A WOMAN WHO FEARS THE LORD IS TO BE PRAISED."
—PROVERBS 31:30

You are beautiful. But you are so much more than that. You are a daughter of God. Contrary to what society may tell you, looking "perfect" is not your life's purpose. As Christians, we're called to a much greater mission- to know, love, and honor God. And how can we do that if we're preoccupied with our outside appearances? As the adage goes, "it's the inside that counts." Dedicating our lives to thinness or food will yield nothing but physical consequences- and often times quite dangerous ones. However, can you imagine the results we get when we dedicate our lives to our Savior and Creator?

Heavenly Father, I praise You for creating me as Your daughter. I long for a relationship with You. Give me the courage and will to set You as the focus of my life, above all earthly things. Your purpose for me was not to lead a life at war with my body; my purpose is so much greater. Make my work clear to me, Lord, so I can better please You.

Activity: Make a list of your best qualities. One rule though- nothing pertaining to your physical self. Just those parts of you that make you... you! Your personality, passions, and talents. Thank God for these gifts.

Day Six

"GOD IS WITHIN HER, SHE WILL NOT FALL; GOD WILL HELP HER AT BREAK OF DAY" —PSALM 46:5

How reassuring is this verse? It allows us the confidence to submit our worries and troubles to God- to trust Him- knowing He will be there to help. Moreover, we learn that the spirit of God is *inside* of us, should we submit to Him and allow Him into our souls. No trouble is too big (or too small!) for God. He is there for us, no questions asked. We seek this support in so many of the wrong places, using all the wrong coping skills. How much better off would we be if we called upon God's strength when we are weak? We could conquer what holds us back. God wants to help you. All you have to do is ask!

✝

Lord, You are my strength when I am weak. Thank You for Your everlasting support for me. I praise You for all of the good You have done in my life. Allow me to see the areas in which You shine through me, so that I may better reflect Your love.

Activity: We all face challenges every day- some easier than others. In the coming day, count how many times you think or say negative things like, "I can't" or "it's too difficult". Because with God, you can conquer anything.

Day Seven

"SO WHETHER YOU EAT OR DRINK OR WHATEVER YOU DO, DO IT ALL FOR THE GLORY OF GOD." – 1 CORINTHIANS 10:31

This verse reminds us that everything we do is for God. Not just church, volunteer work, or prayers. *Everything.* Choosing to eat when you want to restrict honors God. Nourishing your body instead of bingeing honors God. Making the conscious decision to deny your eating disorder and allow your body health and happiness... that makes God grin from ear to ear. Now suppose we honor our eating disorder and deny God's healing power? You guessed it- it weakens our spirits and our bodies. Not to mention our relationship with Him.

Lord Jesus, everything I do, I do for You. Help me to be more conscious of this as I make decisions in my day-to-day life. I ask that You give me the guidance to act according to Your will in all I do.

Activity: Think back upon your day's events. Were there choices you made that were pleasing to God? Any that weren't? Make it a point to be more mindful of your daily decisions and identify how you can align them to be more in tune with God's plan.

_____

_____

_____

_____

_____

_____

_____

_____

_____

_____

_____

_____

_____

_____

_____

_____

_____

_____

_____

_____

_____

_____

Day Eight

"BUT YOU ARE... GOD'S SPECIAL POSSESSION, THAT YOU MAY DECLARE THE PRAISES OF HIM WHO CALLED YOU OUT OF DARKNESS INTO HIS WONDERFUL LIGHT." —1 PETER 2:9

You are special to God. You are His daughter. He is the King above all Kings. Therefore, you are a princess. You deserve the best of the best, as you are part of His royal family. You deserve all of the happiness and peace promised to His people. He will give you that, if you allow Him. What's holding us back isn't a fire-breathing dragon below the tower we've been locked in for a decade. It's the chains of our disorders keeping us from experiencing the fulfillment He promises. Much like the knight in shining armor, God will come to our rescue when we ask.

God, thank You for the love and honor with which You created me. Help me learn to treat myself the way I should be treated- as a princess. You have so much planned for me, Lord; help me break free of these chains so I may better enjoy the life You have given me.

Activity: Take some time out of your schedule to treat yourself. Give yourself a pedicure, make a DIY facial, anything to pamper yourself. You deserve it!

_____

_____

_____

_____

_____

_____

_____

_____

_____

_____

_____

_____

_____

_____

_____

_____

_____

_____

_____

_____

_____

_____

_____

_____

_____

Day Nine

"PEOPLE LOOK AT THE OUTWARD APPEARANCE, BUT THE LORD LOOKS AT THE HEART." — 1 SAMUEL 16:7

How much time do you take to get ready in the morning? Hair, makeup, clothes, 10 minutes? 30? More? Now how long do we spend preparing our *souls* for the day ahead? (Insert audible crickets). Yeah, didn't think so. Most people (myself included) spend unnecessary amounts of time preparing our physical selves, but far too little on our internal selves. God reminds us that He doesn't care if you look a mess or if you're runway ready. He only looks at your heart. That's what's important to Him. It's important to ask ourselves who we're trying to impress— our peers or our Lord?

✢

Heavenly Father, You love me with a love unconditional of my looks. Help me to find that same love for myself. Allow me to forget those troubles so that I may grow closer in relationship with You by bettering my heart, As that's what really matters in Your eyes.

Activity: Use the journal space below to draw two hearts. Let one be your heart while burdened with an eating disorder, and designate the other to be your heart in recovery. What's inside your struggling heart? Pain, self-hatred, sadness? Now picture your heart how you'd like it to be. What would be different?

_____

_____

_____

_____

_____

_____

_____

_____

_____

_____

_____

_____

_____

_____

_____

_____

_____

_____

_____

_____

Day Ten

Unfortunately, Satan knows how to work us quite well. He knows our insecurities, weaknesses, and our troubles, and he works hard to manipulate those. And man, does Satan love a good eating disorder. He can suck the life out of you by depriving your body of its life sources: food and God. It takes immense strength to deny the urges to act on these disordered behaviors. Fortunately, we don't have to do it alone. When we submit to God and allow His help in conquering our demons, we can find solace. Satan runs at the sight of God. Keep Him close by; you're gonna need His graces.

✝

Dear God, You've proven time and time again Your triumph over evil. You have conquered it all. Guide me as I fight off the demons working so hard to put me off track. Keep me close to You that You may protect me from the tricks and lies of my disordered thinking.

Activity: Identify those weaknesses and triggers that cause you to stumble. Pray for the guidance to build up those areas so that you can stand confident in times of struggle, not crumble under the pressure.

_____

_____

_____

_____

_____

_____

_____

_____

_____

_____

_____

_____

_____

_____

_____

_____

_____

_____

_____

_____

_____

_____

Day Eleven

When was the last time you felt free? I mean, *really* free? Free to eat without shame or worry, free to wear the clothes you want without regard to how it makes you look, free to love yourself? For most of us, it's been far too long. We turn to disordered eating as a means of escaping something- an internal pain or struggle. But it turns out, we dig ourselves deeper and deeper into our despair. Have heart! Christ has bought you- yes, you!- the freedom from these chains, so that you might enjoy the simplicity of a life in Him. You *can* find that freedom you long for... so long as you're looking in the right places.

Lord God, You've promised Your children a freedom that no earthly measures can even compare to. Give me the guidance to seek this freedom in You, Lord, not the coping skills I've relied upon for so long. Free me from the chains of my eating disorder so that I may enjoy the full abundance of Your blessings.

Activity: What makes you feel "stuck"? Is it the rules your disorder has established? How about the inability to enjoy your favorite food from childhood? Identify those areas that cause you to feel confined and ask for God's graces so that you may experience the freedom of no longer associating with those troubles.

_____

_____

_____

_____

_____

_____

_____

_____

_____

_____

_____

_____

_____

_____

_____

_____

_____

_____

_____

_____

Day Twelve

"THEREFORE I TELL YOU, DO NOT WORRY ABOUT YOUR LIFE, WHAT YOU WILL EAT OR DRINK; OR ABOUT YOUR BODY, WHAT YOU WILL WEAR. IS NOT LIFE MORE THAN FOOD, AND THE BODY MORE THAN CLOTHES?" —MATTHEW 6:25

Eating disorders are obsessive in nature; they like control. Satan works through those disorders to try and control everything- what you eat, what you wear, how you live your life. But God assures us we needn't worry about those things. Life is so much more than that. Imagine, if you will, a life without those worries that plague you on a daily basis. Pretty sweet, huh? This passage continues in verse 26, saying "Look at the birds of the air; they do not sow or reap or store away in barns, and yet your heavenly Father feeds them" reminding us that God provides for the creatures of the Earth, who do nothing for themselves. This verse finishes by challenging our thoughts, posing the question, "Are you not much more valuable than [the birds]?" (Hint: you are.)

✝

Dear God, I thank You for all that You have provided for me. My family, the food on the table, the clothes I wear, and the roof over my head. Allow me to relinquish all of my worries and anxieties to You, fully trusting that You will take care of me.

Activity: Make a list of the worries that burden your mind and soul. Crumple it, burn it, do whatever you have to in order to symbolize giving all of these things to God. *There isn't anything too big or too small for God.*

_____

_____

_____

_____

_____

_____

_____

_____

_____

_____

_____

_____

_____

_____

_____

_____

_____

_____

_____

_____

_____

_____

_____

Day Thirteen

"I CAN DO ALL THIS THROUGH HIM WHO GIVES ME STRENGTH." —PHILIPPIANS 4:13

Recovery is a long, difficult process. We often get tempted to give up. We become weak. Those moments of weakness are what causes us to relapse. But don't lose hope! God has offered His undying strength to those who believe in Him. After all, He made the world by hand. Don't you think He has the strength to help you conquer your demons? God doesn't want us to do it alone; He wants to lift us up so we can live freely again. He wants to take every last burden off of our shoulders into His hands so that we can experience a life free of worries.

✝

Lord, You are almighty and powerful, Alpha and Omega. Take these worries off my shoulders. Help me to move the mountains of my disorder with Your strength. You have the strength that I can't do without. Give me the humility to offer my troubles up to You, and give me the strength to persevere in this battle.

Activity: What are your areas of weakness? Where do you make excuses? Identify these areas of your life, and ask God's blessing over them. Pray that He grants you the strength to conquer them.

_____

_____

_____

_____

_____

_____

_____

_____

_____

_____

_____

_____

_____

_____

_____

_____

_____

_____

_____

_____

_____

_____

_____

Day Fourteen

"So do not throw away your confidence; it will be richly rewarded. You need to persevere so that when you have done the will of God, you will receive what He has promised." —Hebrews 10:35-36

How many times do you look in the mirror and like what you see? I mean, *really* like. If you're like most of us, those days come few and far in between. Whether it's a matter of body image or self-esteem, we don't always feel entirely self-confident. To add to the trouble, we, as Christians, are told not to take pride in ourselves. So what's a girl to do? Finding your confidence, not in physical matters, but in Godly matters is a nice happy medium. When we become confident in ourselves, not because our jeans look stellar or our hair is just right, but because we are God's creation, we get to experience the life and love He has promised us.

Lord God, You crafted me with such love and care. Help me see the best in myself that You are responsible for. Give me the courage to feel confident in myself because I am made in Your image, not for worldly reasons. Allow me the peace in knowing I'm made just as You intended.

Activity: The next time you stand in front of the mirror, stop yourself from criticizing your appearance. Instead, find *three* nice things about yourself that identify *you* as a child of God.

_____

_____

_____

_____

_____

_____

_____

_____

_____

_____

_____

_____

_____

_____

_____

_____

_____

_____

_____

_____

_____

_____

_____

Day Fifteen

"...WHATEVER IS TRUE, WHATEVER IS NOBLE, WHATEVER IS RIGHT, WHATEVER IS PURE, WHATEVER IS LOVELY, WHATEVER IS ADMIRABLE—IF ANYTHING IS EXCELLENT OR PRAISEWORTHY—THINK ABOUT SUCH THINGS." — PHILIPPIANS 4:8

What does your internal dialogue sound like? Are you mostly thinking positive thoughts about yourself? Or do you find that you're regularly putting yourself down? In this passage of scripture, Paul reminds us to keep our eyes- and minds- on the prize: a life in harmony with God. How do we expect to live a life recovered from disordered eating if we allow our minds to entertain the disordered thoughts? These thought patterns are destructive. They aren't true, noble, right, pure, lovely, admirable- they keep us from God. We shouldn't allow those thoughts to stay.

✝

Heavenly Father, I praise You for the intellect You have given me, and the ability to think, feel, and make choices. Help me to use this gift to honor You, and not allow disordered thoughts to plague my mind. Give me the strength to clear my mind of these thoughts so that I may better focus on You.

Activity: In the upcoming days, try to be very conscious of the thoughts that you allow into your mind. Use Paul's test (are these thoughts true, noble, right, pure, lovely, admirable) to decide if these thoughts are worth your time and energy.

_____

_____

_____

_____

_____

_____

_____

_____

_____

_____

_____

_____

_____

_____

_____

_____

_____

_____

_____

_____

_____

Day Sixteen

"SOME... SUFFERED AFFLICTION BECAUSE OF THEIR INIQUITIES. THEY LOATHED ALL FOOD AND DREW NEAR THE GATES OF DEATH. THEN THEY CRIED TO THE LORD IN THEIR TROUBLE, AND HE SAVED THEM FROM THEIR DISTRESS." —
PSALM 107:17-19

If this verse doesn't give us a clear-cut message on recovering, I don't know what does. When we suffer the afflictions of an eating disorder, we become fearful. Certain foods will trigger us to restrict, to binge, to purge. All of these habits have dire- and sometimes even fatal-consequences. While the writer of this Psalm didn't specify who "they" refers to, we can apply this to our own struggles. The longer we remain in the confines of disordered eating, the nearer we draw to the "gates of death" mentioned here. But there is hope! The people who struggled with this loathing of food cried out to the Lord, asking for His help and graces. And what did He do? He saved them, just as He promised.

✝

Dear God, Your saving powers can be traced all through history. You promise freedom and, when we call, You deliver. Give me the courage to reach out to You in my times of doubt and struggle. Lift me with Your loving hand out of the darkness and into the light.

Activity: Identify which areas of disordered eating burden you the most. Pray for the guidance to recognize triggers as they appear, and remember to call on God when you feel temped to rely on unhealthy means of coping with discomfort.

_____

_____

_____

_____

_____

_____

_____

_____

_____

_____

_____

_____

_____

_____

_____

_____

_____

_____

_____

_____

_____

_____

Day Seventeen

"THEREFORE, AS GOD'S CHOSEN PEOPLE... CLOTHE YOURSELVES WITH COMPASSION, KINDNESS, HUMILITY, GENTLENESS AND PATIENCE... AND OVER ALL THESE VIRTUES PUT ON LOVE." – COLOSSIANS 3:12,14

The daily dilemma of what to wear. Chances are, you find yourself stuck in this every now and then. And if you're like me, it can be a bit of an ordeal. When we have a distorted sense of self-image, we try to put value on ourselves by the clothes we wear. We accentuate the parts we like, hide the parts we don't, or sport the big-name clothing brands as if the price tag affects our own worth. And where does that lead us? Probably to feeling self-conscious, insecure, or doubting our self-worth. But why should it? The clothes we wear aren't who we are. Sure, they can *speak* for our values and individuality, but it's those intangible things that *we* ultimately decide. Putting on compassion and gentleness in the morning will get you much farther than those top-dollar boots ever will. Why do we fuss over those material goods, when there is so much more to speak for us?

Dear God, You give me the ability to reach people every day through my words and actions. Give me the confidence to focus more on the spiritual assets I wear rather than the materialistic ones. Allow me the wisdom to honor You in my daily walk.

Activity: The next time you get dressed, visualize yourself putting on these graces- compassion, kindness, humility, gentleness, patience, and love- with each article of clothing. Be mindful, remembering these intentions throughout your day as you encounter challenges.

_____

_____

_____

_____

_____

_____

_____

_____

_____

_____

_____

_____

_____

_____

_____

_____

_____

_____

_____

_____

_____

_____

_____

Day Eighteen

"'LOVE YOUR NEIGHBOR AS YOURSELF.' THERE IS NO
COMMANDMENT GREATER THAN THESE." —MARK 12:31

Jesus tells us that His most important commandment to us is to love one another. Not to love them as we wish to be loved, (this isn't the golden rule!), but to love others as we love ourselves. Now here's the million dollar question- how much is that, exactly? Do we love ourselves enough to speak kindly of ourselves? To give ourselves nourishment when we're hungry? Doing these things for family and friends is a no-brainer, but it's not so easy when the tables are turned. The truth is, we can't fully love those around us if we don't love ourselves. We can't give away something we don't have!

Lord, You've called me not only to love, but to be loved. Thank You for those people in my life who show me the kindness and mercy I often don't show myself. Help me to love myself just as You've made me, so that I might better love those around me.

Activity: Who do you love in your life? This could be a friend, a family member, a pet- anyone to whom you freely show love. Now imagine yourself treating them how you treat yourself, talking to them as you talk to yourself. What would change?

_____

_____

_____

_____

_____

_____

_____

_____

_____

_____

_____

_____

_____

_____

_____

_____

_____

_____

_____

_____

_____

_____

Day Nineteen

"WE HAVE THIS HOPE AS AN ANCHOR FOR THE SOUL, FIRM AND SECURE." —HEBREWS 6:19

Sometimes we feel like we're drowning in all of the stress, worries, and troubles of life. When the waves are crashing down and the boat is rocking, we often get tempted to rely on our old and unhealthy coping mechanisms. Whether we sink or swim depends on who we put our faith in- ourselves, or God. Instead of anchoring ourselves in restriction, binging, or purging, God calls us to anchor ourselves in Him and His promises. Remember—your lifeguard walks on water!

Lord, when the seas of recovery are stormy and I am tempted to seek stability in my old ways, inspire me to instead lean on You. Guide me through the waters so that I may not sink deeper into illness, but instead traverse safely and securely into recovery.

Activity: Who are the rocks or anchors God has blessed you with in your life? Perhaps you can lean on a close friend, a parent, or a therapist. Reach out to them in the coming days and thank them for their support and influence in your spiritual and recovery journeys. Ask that they pray for your continued success in these areas.

_____

_____

_____

_____

_____

_____

_____

_____

_____

_____

_____

_____

_____

_____

_____

_____

_____

_____

_____

_____

_____

Day Twenty

"ALL THE DAYS OF THE OPPRESSED ARE WRETCHED, BUT THE CHEERFUL HEART HAS A CONTINUAL FEAST." PROVERBS 15:15

Despite the way in which our culture has romanticized eating disorders, the reality of the illnesses is far less glamorous. To use Solomon's words from this verse in Proverbs, the days are "wretched" under the oppressive forces of our eating disorders. However, when we allow God to work in and on our hearts and accept His invitation to a healthier life, we are promised happier days. It is not always easy, but the rewards promised to us far surpass the false security provided by our disorders. All we are asked to do is to trust and rely on Him in the process.

Heavenly Father, You have seen me thorough the darkest days of my illness. Please soften my heart to Your works so that I may fully enjoy the health and happiness promised to me beyond my eating disorder. Help me to grow a cheerful heart in Your presence all my days.

Activity: What are your reasons to recover? Are you motivated by being able to safely enjoy a favorite food again or someday being an inspiration to others in this journey? Jot down a few things you look forward to along the path of recovery and look back at that list when times get tough.

_____

_____

_____

_____

_____

_____

_____

_____

_____

_____

_____

_____

_____

_____

_____

_____

_____

_____

_____

_____

_____

_____

Day Twenty One

You are *not* your body. You *live in* your body. That body is a gift from God, as a house for your soul and as a home for your spirit. Let me say that again for emphasis- *your body is a gift.* And what an amazing gift to have received! It was designed just for you by the ultimate Creator, totally one-of-a-kind. Every freckle, hair, and spot was placed there by God. We're told very clearly to treat it well! It is, after all, where the Holy Spirit lives inside of us. Why then do we not treat it as such? We abuse our bodies so terribly in the midst of our eating disorders that we lose sight of the very purpose of our bodies—not as an object meant to look attractive for others' enjoyment, but a vessel through which the Holy Spirit can work in the world around us.

Thank You, Heavenly Father, for the gift of my body. I recognize that everything about it is Your handiwork. As I learn to take care of this gift, please help me to see myself as You do, as a beautiful piece of this universe rather than something to be changed. Let Your Spirit work through me as You planned.

Activity: Draw your body. Be as detailed or general as you'd like. On the areas you often criticize, write something positive instead. For example, you may write *"I love my thighs because they carry me with every step I take"*. See the purpose in yourself. You are worth more than just your appearance.

_____

_____

_____

_____

_____

_____

_____

_____

_____

_____

_____

_____

_____

_____

_____

_____

_____

_____

_____

_____

_____

_____

_____

Day Twenty Two

"LIVE IN HARMONY WITH ONE ANOTHER. DO NOT BE PROUD... DO NOT BE CONCEITED." —ROMANS 12:16

We live in a society driven by competition and comparison. We worry about who is the "thinnest" or "prettiest" or "most likely to succeed". Sometimes, our disorders may even cause us to worry if we are "sick enough" to validate our feelings and the help we seek out. These superlatives do nothing but cause us to feel insecure and insignificant. See, we *are* enough for Him. He has redeemed each and every one of us regardless of our social status. Not only is this comparison unproductive, but it goes against God's explicit orders to work together. We aren't meant to compare ourselves to one another, but to work alongside each other, building one another up instead of tearing each other down.

✝

Thank You, Dear Lord, for redeeming me on the cross. You deemed me worthy of redemption knowing full well my flaws and imperfections. Help me to accept Your gift of redemption with grace and gratitude. Allow me to make peace with myself and others to live more harmoniously in Your world.

Activity: I challenge you to look yourself in the eyes and repeat this: *I am enough*. How does it feel? Does it feel forced? Fake? Try it a few more times. When your mind begins to challenge what you are saying, remember you do not need to justify it by earthly measures. We have been redeemed. That is all the validation you need.

Day Twenty Three

"BE ON YOUR GUARD; STAND FIRM IN THE FAITH; BE COURAGEOUS; BE STRONG." — 1 JAMES 16:13

We never know what kind of triggers life can throw at us. In what seems like an instant, a beautiful day in recovery can turn into an unexpected battle within our minds. While we can never be 100% prepared for life's surprises, having a solid foundation in our faith provides us with a place to turn when these internal conflicts come up. Be it an unexpected urge to restrict, to binge, or to purge, knowing with all certainty that we have the Lord of Everything fighting alongside us can certainly help us battle the internal demons whenever they arise.

God, as I face the upcoming day, equip me to be able to handle any situation that may arise. Grant me the graces to hold You in my heart so as to win any battles I may face today. Thank You for Your constant support.

Activity: What's in your box of spiritual ammunition? Compile a list of a few go-to scripture verses on an index card to carry around with you as a reminder to pray next time you are faced with unexpected urges.

_____

_____

_____

_____

_____

_____

_____

_____

_____

_____

_____

_____

_____

_____

_____

_____

_____

_____

_____

_____

_____

Day Twenty Four

"COME TO ME, ALL YOU WHO ARE WEARY AND BURDENED, AND I WILL GIVE YOU REST." —MATTHEW 11:28

What a beautiful thing it is to be loved by a God offering such a promise of respite. Knowing we can turn to Him and cast all our worries and anxieties upon Him is such a comforting feeling, but it can be a challenge as well. When things go wrong at home, work, school, or relationships, it can easily become habitual to turn to your eating disorder first. It takes a conscious effort to call upon the Lord in these times. However, knowing He will not let you down nor cause you harm allows us to look forward to His comfort and compassion when we call upon His name.

Dear Lord, I praise You and thank You for Your promises of peace. Allow my soul to rest and heal in Your presence as You guide me along my recovery journey. When it becomes difficult to fight, remind me to seek solace In You. Wrap Your loving arms around me as I face each day and the challenges within it.

Activity: Allow yourself some quiet or meditative time. Be still and listen for His voice as you meditate on this verse of scripture. Breathe deeply and relax as you fill your heart and mind with His word.

_____

_____

_____

_____

_____

_____

_____

_____

_____

_____

_____

_____

_____

_____

_____

_____

_____

_____

_____

_____

_____

_____

_____

Day Twenty Five

"BLESSED IS THE ONE WHO PERSEVERES UNDER TRIAL
BECAUSE, HAVING STOOD THE TEST, THAT PERSON WILL
RECEIVE THE CROWN OF LIFE THAT THE LORD HAS
PROMISED TO THOSE WHO LOVE HIM." —JAMES 1:12

Recovery is a journey. There is no magical fix; it is making a choice, each and every day, to choose life and freedom over the false promises of your eating disorder. The journey is full of trials, but through persevering day in and day out, it becomes more second nature. The urges become more manageable, the triggers less disruptive, the lapses fewer and farther between. We as Christians are promised great things through our choices to follow God, be it in day-to-day life or the recovery process. We can look forward to a life of freedom by putting in the work and continually asking His blessings as we march on.

✝

Lord God, You have brought me this far in my journey of recovery. It has been difficult, but You have not left my side. Thank You for Your presence in this life-changing path I walk. Give me the graces to continue to persevere no matter how trying it gets. Lift me up so that I may experience a life free from the chains of my eating disorder.

Activity: What is your recovery mantra? Identify a verse of scripture or a phrase to repeat when facing a trial or trigger. Write on the following page and spend a few minutes reflecting on what it means to you in your journey.

_____

_____

_____

_____

_____

_____

_____

_____

_____

_____

_____

_____

_____

_____

_____

_____

_____

_____

_____

_____

_____

Day Twenty Six

"HE GIVES STRENGTH TO THE WEARY AND INCREASES THE POWER OF THE WEAK." —ISAIAH 40:29

Eating disorders are a destructive class of illnesses. They wreak havoc on us physically, emotionally, and spiritually, leaving us exhausted and vulnerable to their vicious cycles. Though proper nutrition can sometimes be all that is needed to restore our physical health, spiritual and emotional health are not always as quick to follow in the recovery process. (On the other hand, it is in strengthening these areas that we become better able to maintain progress in recovery). God promises us these things when we turn to Him in times of trouble. In our weakness, we are encouraged to seek His help and rely on Him for strength. It is only through Him that we can overcome our disorders and rise above the cycle of self-destruction.

Lord, You know the areas in which I struggle. While I work to regain my physical health, lay Your hands on me and restore my emotional and spiritual wellbeing. Strengthen me with Your power so that I may stand strong in the face of my eating disorder. Thank You for Your continued blessing on my recovery.

Activity: In what areas do you find yourself in most need of strength? Is it your body image that causes you to stumble? Do you find impulsivity to be a weak spot? Identify this area in your life and ask God for guidance in strengthening it. Write down a game plan for tackling an issue in this area to have on hand the next time a struggle arises.

_____

_____

_____

_____

_____

_____

_____

_____

_____

_____

_____

_____

_____

_____

_____

_____

_____

_____

_____

_____

_____

_____

_____

Day Twenty Seven

"BECAUSE HE HIMSELF SUFFERED WHEN HE WAS TEMPTED, HE IS ABLE TO HELP THOSE WHO ARE BEING TEMPTED." —HEBREWS 2:18

Though fully God, we as Christians believe Jesus to be fully man as well. He too faced temptation and struggle in His time on Earth. (You can read more about it in Matthew chapter 4, verses 1-11). Though perfect and infallible, Jesus is not unsympathetic to the feeling of temptation. He truly understands what we feel when faced with urges from our disorders because He has experienced it. Likewise, He knows how to help and support us in those times. How encouraging it is to know that we are not alone.

✝

Lord Jesus, You left Your seat at the Throne of God to live as a man on Earth. You know firsthand the feeling of temptation because You experienced it Yourself. Help me, Lord, as I face temptations to lapse into my eating disorder. Strengthen me so that I may rise above as You did.

Activity: Flip open your Bible to Matthew and read chapter 4, verses 1-11. What can we learn about resisting our own eating disorder urges by reading Jesus's experiences with temptation? Write down any insights you have on your journal page.

_____

_____

_____

_____

_____

_____

_____

_____

_____

_____

_____

_____

_____

_____

_____

_____

_____

_____

_____

_____

_____

_____

_____

_____

Day Twenty Eight

"BECAUSE OF THE LORD'S GREAT LOVE WE ARE NOT CONSUMED, FOR HIS COMPASSIONS NEVER FAIL. THEY ARE NEW EVERY MORNING; GREAT IS YOUR FAITHFULNESS." — LAMENTATIONS 3:22-33

When it feels like your eating disorder has taken over your life, this verse can be exceptionally reassuring. Though a major part of our personal stories, our illnesses are not our destiny. Because of His love, we have the power and potential to rise to so much more. Each day we are offered a brand new start at reshaping our future to one of health and freedom. No matter your past, our Lord allows you the free will to take the reins and steer your life in a new direction. There is hope because of His love and faithfulness.

✝

Heavenly Father, thank You for the gift of this new day. Your great love and compassion give me hope as I strive towards freedom from my eating disorder. Today I ask Your graces in my journey so that this day may be a fresh start. Walk with me, Lord, as I continue to travel the path of recovery.

Activity: What is the first thing you do in the morning? Do you instantly reach for your phone to check up on social media? Set a reminder on your phone to spend the first five minutes of the next new day in prayer. You may be surprised at how this simple act can set the tone for the day ahead.

_____

_____

_____

_____

_____

_____

_____

_____

_____

_____

_____

_____

_____

_____

_____

_____

_____

_____

_____

_____

_____

Day Twenty Nine

"DO NOT BE AFRAID. STAND FIRM AND YOU WILL SEE THE DELIVERANCE THE LORD WILL BRING YOU TODAY." – EXODUS 14:13

Moses spoke these words to the Israelites (who at that time were slaves of the Egyptians) as they feared for their liberation from the oppression they faced. Moses, however, trusted God and His promises to release them from captivity. His faith in God was not futile; they eventually were led out of Egypt and were freed from the chains of slavery. Likewise, we are promised deliverance from the chains of our eating disorders. It takes hard work and great faith on our part, but God will not leave us helpless, just as He did not abandon Moses and the Israelites.

✝

God, we have seen Your works through the Bible and the freedom You grant to Your people in whatever hardships they face. Free me, Lord, from the shackles of my eating disorder so I may be better able to serve You. Help me to trust in You regardless of how hopeless things may seem.

Activity: Draw a picture of your chains. Write on them all that keeps you from living life to the fullest. Offer these things up to God in prayer and ask that He release you from these burdens.

_____

_____

_____

_____

_____

_____

_____

_____

_____

_____

_____

_____

_____

_____

_____

_____

_____

_____

_____

_____

_____

_____

_____

Day Thirty

"THE LIGHT SHINES IN THE DARKNESS, AND THE DARKNESS HAS NOT OVERCOME IT." —JOHN 1:5

No matter how hopeless we may feel, how broken we perceive ourselves, how dire our situations, there will always be a hope for those who trust in God. He, who created darkness and light, never has and will never be defeated by the darkness. Like the bright moon in the night sky or the candle in a dark room, the Lord will always be there to help us find our way out. If we seek Him, we will find Him. He will help us to overcome.

Heavenly Father, there has never been a moment in my life in which You have not been by my side. Help me to seek and to feel Your presence each day as I battle my eating disorder. Remind me that I am never alone; You are always with me.

Activity: Where do you feel God's presence most in your life? This could be a physical location, such as in nature, or an activity like spending time with loved ones. Journal about those experiences, and make it a point to spend more time where you feel Him most.

_____

_____

_____

_____

_____

_____

_____

_____

_____

_____

_____

_____

_____

_____

_____

_____

_____

_____

_____

_____

_____

_____

Day Thirty One

"JESUS SAID, 'IF YOU HOLD TO MY TEACHING, YOU ARE REALLY MY DISCIPLES. THEN YOU WILL KNOW THE TRUTH, AND THE TRUTH WILL SET YOU FREE.'" —JOHN 8:31-32

What do you know to be true? You have been saved. You have been redeemed. You are fearfully and wonderfully made. Believing these truths—*really* believing them and all they hold, will equip you with the strength and power to recover. You will see your worth, your value, and your individuality. You will be unstoppable. With the Lord beside you and this knowledge within you, you can and will be set free from your eating disorder.

You, Lord, are what I hold to be true. With Your teachings as my guide and Your words as my hope, I ask that You be with me as I continue my path to health and happiness. May my happiness rest in You, Lord, and not on worldly things. Grant me freedom from my eating disorder and a life fully in Your presence.

Activity: What truths have you learned on this journey to recovery? Perhaps you've seen just how strong you can be with God in your life, or discovered a newfound respect for how He made you. Take a moment to write these down so that you can reflect on them in the days ahead.

_____

_____

_____

_____

_____

_____

_____

_____

_____

_____

_____

_____

_____

_____

_____

_____

_____

_____

_____

_____

_____

_____

ABOUT THE AUTHOR

Caitlyn Hoerner has sought to inspire others through her writing from the young age of thirteen, when she was selected to publish her first piece of poetry in a national anthology. Caitlyn has since published total of seven poems. Now, after having overcome her own struggles with an eating disorder, Caitlyn seeks to lead others out of the chains of illness and into a life of recovery, with God on their side. Taking the skills she has learned through her journey and armed with the Word of God, Caitlyn hopes to show others that they, too, are *wonderfully made.*

`

RESOURCES

If you or a loved one is struggling with an eating disorder, please visit the following resources to find support and services in your area.

National Eating Disorders Association
Online: www.nationaleatingdisorders.org
Helpline: 1-800-931-2237

National Alliance on Mental Illness
Online: www.nami.org
Phone: 800-950-NAMI; Text "NAMI" to 741741

Made in the USA
Middletown, DE
07 September 2024

60528446R00042